About the Author

Taylor Balfour is a writer, editor, poet, and creative based in Regina, Saskatchewan. Her lifelong dream has been to be a published author. She loves bunnies, sushi, Taylor Swift, and a good cup of coffee.

This is a work of creative non-fiction. The events are portrayed to the best of the author's memory. While all the stories in this book are true, some names and identifying details have been changed to protect the privacy of the people involved.

At Least We'll Always Have Spring

Taylor Balfour

At Least We'll Always Have Spring

Vanguard Press

VANGUARD PAPERBACK

© Copyright 2024
Taylor Balfour

The right of Taylor Balfour to be identified as author of
this work has been asserted by her in accordance with the
Copyright, Designs and Patents Act 1988.

All Rights Reserved

No reproduction, copy or transmission of this publication
may be made without written permission.
No paragraph of this publication may be reproduced,
copied or transmitted save with the written permission of the
publisher, or in accordance with the provisions
of the Copyright Act 1956 (as amended).

Any person who commits any unauthorised act in relation to
this publication may be liable to criminal
prosecution and civil claims for damages.

A CIP catalogue record for this title is
available from the British Library.

ISBN 978 1 83794 180 3

*Vanguard Press is an imprint of
Pegasus Elliot Mackenzie Publishers Ltd.*
www.pegasuspublishers.com

First Published in 2024

**Vanguard Press
Sheraton House Castle Park
Cambridge England**

Printed & Bound in Great Britain

To Rachel, my sister and best friend. I hope I've made you proud. This is for you. I hope I'm making you proud. Everything I do is for you. I love you.

Thank you to my mom and dad, Heather and Jim, for believing in me. Thank you for believing I could accomplish my dream. Thank you to my friends: Kelly, Madi, Jane, Mason, Abi, Abby, Maighen, Dellrae, Oakley, Tamara, Lindsay, Hayleigh, Braedon Brittney and Angelica. I couldn't have been here without your love. Thank you, thank you, thank you. You've helped my dream become a reality.

Introduction

February fifth 2019 was, and will forever be, the worst day of my life. Waking up that day at my then-boyfriend's house, I remember thinking: *I wish I could sleep for a few more hours*. But I kissed him goodbye, grabbed my bookbag full of textbooks and notebooks, and I drove to campus.

I was groggy. After all, he and I had been playing a version of *Dungeons and Dragons* with friends (yes, we were that couple) until almost four a.m.

By the time I landed on campus, about fifteen minutes before my class was set to begin, I avoided doing homework by, instead, scrolling through Facebook. I specifically remember sharing a Facebook post about Beyblades (don't ask) right before I received the text that still haunts me to this day.

'Have you heard from your sister?'

It was from my dad.

The answer was no, I hadn't. The last time I spoke to her was on Friday, almost four days prior, via text. It was about the Netflix password. I had been out that night, with friends at a student film party on campus, and responded whenever I had a chance.

I didn't think much of the text initially. I responded that I'd check in with her and did exactly that, shooting her a 'Yo dude, how's life?' while getting set up in class.

But the longer class droned on, and the longer I saw that I hadn't received a response from her, a pit in my stomach began to grow.

Class ended an hour and fifteen minutes later, and I headed straight home. Once I arrived, I noticed Mom's car parked in the garage: her purple Honda CRV. It was a sign that she had taken the day off of work and came home. It was a rarity. It made the pit in my stomach grow more.

I found her in her bedroom, weeping at her desk. She was in the middle of buying last minute tickets to Edmonton to visit my sister, Rachel.

"I think something's wrong," my mother said at the time. "I don't think she's well."

My dad came home half an hour later. All of us had still heard nothing.

I tried to eat, but I couldn't stomach anything. I tried to take a bath, but it only made me more anxious. I even began scouring her university's subreddit on Reddit, knowing that she frequented the forum and that it was constantly up to date on campus happenings. Two separate posts on the home page acknowledged an apparent suicide in Rachel's dorm building. I turned off my phone and prayed that it was someone else.

The police arrived after two p.m., two officers and two members from victims services. They comforted us while we screamed, and cried, and while I watched my parents fall apart for the first and only time in my entire life.

"I'm sorry, Mrs Balfour, but your daughter has been found dead."

They notified us that Rachel had been found dead in her university dorm room. She was laying in bed with her headphones on. She had been left there, undiscovered, for almost four days. The last time I had spoken to her, the very night I was occupied at a student film party, was the night she presumably died.

Rachel was my best friend. She was a blonde-haired, blue-eyed bucket of spunk. None of us would've had it any other way. She loved Coke Slurpees and hated wearing her glasses. She adored animation and wanted to pursue it as a side career, but her real passion was in computer science and coding. She was going to school majoring in computer science, one of very few women in the field. Despite these successes, and despite her passionate, hard-working nature, she struggled with depression and anxiety.

Rachel was a straight-A student and routinely landed on the honour roll. She loved dogs, and had a soft spot for volunteering. Her activism resided largely in advocating for the homeless, and fighting for better, more widely available, and affordable mental health services for all.

She died from opiate poisoning, from taking drugs laced with fentanyl, which inevitably resulted in her overdose and death. It was ruled as an accident.

Months after her death, we received her autopsy and toxicology report in the mail. It found that she had taken a combination of methamphetamine and heroin which had been laced, unknowingly to her, with fentanyl. This method of death is known as opiate poisoning, as the user has died from something laced within the substance that the user isn't aware of.

Rachel was beautiful, inside and out, but she struggled mentally like so many in our world do. Before her death, she had been placed on wait lists for counselling at her university; she had reached out (to no avail) to ask university staff for academic support regarding scheduling her classes. She was more than a province away from home. She was alone. She was desperate. She had no healthy coping strategy left that would leave her feeling safe, sane, and okay.

She was killed. She was preyed upon when at her most vulnerable. I can't bear to imagine her last moments. Was she afraid? Did she know what was happening to her? Did she fall asleep peacefully? Or was she aware of every tiny feeling in her body? These questions, will haunt me, for the rest of my life. I will never come to know what happened in that dorm room in the early hours of that Saturday. That, in itself, breaks my heart.

Rachel died in the thick of our Canadian winter. Not only were we in the midst of a polar vortex (resulting in it being -50 degrees celsius on the daily) but I felt stuck in that perpetual winter for all of 2019. The world felt cold and distant, dreary, and dead. The earth was hidden under a blanket of white, hiding the flowers, sending away the birds, and isolating us from our loved ones.

A few months into counselling, my counsellor asked me, "What does it feel like when you feel seen or understood?"

I responded with, "Yellow and warm."

Suddenly, everything clicked.

Yellow, warm sunlight. The blooming of flowers and the budding of spring. Rebirth. Regrowth. Finding hope after decay. Shedding one's old life and entering a new one.

After Rachel died, I lost many close friends. My boyfriend left me, my academic grades suffered, and many friends and loved ones didn't understand what was happening with me, and stopped talking to me. My world was collapsing around me. Back then, winter was at its peak.

But time has passed. I have written letters to every decaying piece of my life, nurturing it back to health. I have rebuilt my self-esteem, my friendship circle, and my purpose. I have sowed seeds of healing, and they have bloomed. The decay is long gone. The fall has arrived and left. Summer has come through time and peace.

Spring has finally arrived. I'm so excited to finally share her with you.

Thank you for hearing me, like so few did. But most of all, thank you to my sister. You gave me a life I could've only dreamed of.

I hope you enjoy my spring.

Winter

Goodbye

My dearest sweet pea,
I am the hole in the snow outside—
the vacant space where feeling once was.
My fading sunshine, I'm sorry.

There are trenches in the backyard, a trauma
inherited; our crown. I cry,
and I try, but this gouge
will never be whole. I bury and bury hoping
that when it is gone
we can pretend.

I have tried but I can't visit
for a while. There are seasons I must
help breathe. Mother Nature
needs her daughter. Now,
when the snow melts,
it is up to me.

The earth is crying, and I can't
make my world
feel less cold.
I have been trying to come home, to see
you
but the stars
demand
that I stay.

Until my eyes bid goodnight and
my heart is steeped in earth, I will sit
here with autumn and spring
waiting for the shift
in the snow.

The Second Anniversary

My dearest Rachel,

I can't grasp that you're ash in the living room. You're sealed in stone and wrapped in ribbons; a good day and long night. How long has it been since I called you? Since I heard you? Or since I touched your slight hand? How long? How many hours? Minutes? I've felt them all. Polaroids bleed over time. A smile with a firecracker. Our childhood dog. Their paint lingers where I cannot.

The living room is a stranger and I'm afraid to ask her name. There are ridges in the wall from thrown knives, words tossed without regard. The carpet sponges up our regrets. I feel them, dead petals between my toes.

Hers is an old friendship, one I do not wish to rekindle. Her skin snaps every twig on my timeline. Her smile is the lock on the front door, and her presence makes the walls feel

old. They live longer than the twigs in the yard, the heartbeat in the raspberry bush, or the tomb in the basement. Every room feels like a ghost, but the living room is a haunting, and I am lost. The walls close and cave.

The room needs a name change.

There's poison on the walls. The paint cries, the concrete shivers, and I miss not the living room, but the dead driveway. Your heartbeat stuck to my palm, a sticky note on the highway. Your laugh is a promise against my windshield. Frost creeps on your side, a victim to the chill of time. She has set pinpoints on a foreign highway. Electric, she is the psalm of wintertide. With the glow of '75 on the radio, our crimson couch was

an afterthought. I wish on dead stars, but they're gone by the time I am free.

There is an ache in my windshield. A dull hum, withered and weathered, that drinks in the evening like whiskey. The cosmos thrums in the night, a ricochet, a sign that she is home. The side of the highway, an epiphany. But to them, you

are static and quiet. You are still,

hidden.

Rubatosis

I have been waiting for this day. Tonight, I fall
into my skin, the bittersweet cave, down
into a universe painting me purple.
I wish it didn't. These lips are sealed. I melt,
ready for the world to begin its fade.
I can't wait to be pushing up daisies.

It's been haunting all day. That sound. The daisies,
they will soon litter my bedside. The fall
of a family, the scorching of blonde strands, the fade
of that rhythmic curse. I wear purple
like ink stains on my being. Should it be blue? I melt.
Do you hear me? I'm on my way down.

I'm hugging silence to my chest all the way down.
But I hear her, whispering within me, so softly the daisies
begin to sway. Make her be quiet. The melting
of the snow is moons away, and the fall
of autumn is in eons. I wonder if they'll still be blue
when nature's death is so far. It's time. Let's fade.

She's louder now. The sky that made
me is calling. Weeping. Her tears run down
the window's glass. It doesn't matter. The pink
that won't call me home. Will the lilies? Or the daisies

Mom likes to break, snapping their necks, watching their fall
    to the floor, while noticing the cards she's been dealt.

They'll hate me. My father will smelt
    his life into something better. Something that may fade
    along with me. A sunset. A cold sestina. The fall
    of spring; our empire. He pushes me, burying, all the way down.
    I can't wait to be pushing up daisies.
    My lips are already painting purple.

    I hate these shades of ruin. I'm draped in blue silks;
    the ones that flush my skin like buzzing tea leaves. I melt
    into the tapestry. Do you think they'll remember me? The roses?
    The way they fall into oceans, how they fade
    over time, breaking free, just like me; petals all the way down.
    But, remind me, why did I want to fall?

    I've lost it all.
    My skin blooms like heathers, purple,
    pained. My clothes are a chilled canvas, my frown
    and heart, dismantled. It is done. I am empty in all I've felt.

My steady company has left me. But why? Am I fading?

I thought I couldn't wait to push up daisies.

Nothing More Than a Tombstone

"When you die, your name goes on a tombstone and will be forgotten."
No.

The gear shift is a dagger. I snap it to park. Her blonde hair nods with honesty. A fog on a moor, she's ever-looming but untouchable. Her words were all that ever landed.

What about her sister? Her dog? Her friends? The stranger who retained her ten a.m. kindness, a large black coffee on a chilly March day. Her smile has been broken and scattered. What about all those that have found fragments?

The paintings linger in the library, tattooing her legacy into the walls. They too have lost their creator. Are they unable to miss her as well?

"Once you die, there's nothing tangible to remember."
But her skin wasn't all that died.

Her laugh is stuck in the basement stairwell, spilled all over the walls. It is all we have left. Walkways, highways, cafes, and streets, her face is a haze in every crowd.

She looked at me sideways, the car air growing stale. Her voice is an hourglass, sands slipping away. I can only watch.

"Do you have the keys?"
"Yeah, I'll grab the door."

Her body, eight feet deep,

will never tell us why.

the span of a year

8.29.18
You hated Tuesdays and the colour
blue, and told me the sunset tasted like
sweet tequila. I wished for tea.

11.10.18
I begin my novel with you
across the table from me. You laugh
at the crinkle of my nose when the foam of my coffee
grasps my tongue. The cafe is warm, a hug from all sides—
a warning wrapped in
an apology.

2.2.19
The sky took you in blankets, tucked
in the nook of a bookshelf, lost in the ink
of a four-year-old letter. I pour myself another glass of wine,
my laughs dressed in lace on the crimson carpet,
as you suffocate in four paper walls
and a dream.

2.5.19
I see the man in the bulletproof vest
haunting the bottom of the stairs. I faint

when he says "I'm so sorry,"

0.0.00
My mother's hug clutches my blue shoulders, and
in the cups Mom wants to break, I drink tequila like water
hoping it will bring me
closer
to you.

2.5.19, 2:05p.m.
The police knock at the door, and the carpet is stained
with sunlight. The water in the tap doesn't taste just right,
and we take the coffee mugs from the kitchen's cupboard
and bury them in the concrete.

2.6.19
Mom and Dad don't know that I know.

2.7.19
I don't even know if you do.

2.2.19
They say
you had your headphones on.
Your veins must have danced too vapidly, and collapsed

from the weight of drums. It was how you wanted to go.

Mom and Dad don't need to know that.

2.8.19
I find our childhood necklaces, infinite
and tangled at the back of my desk.
They've grown dusty,
and I hate myself.

2.9.19
I won't tell anyone.

3.26.19
I step into your room, taste your electricity,
and leave before the code crackles.

2.4.19
You were left there for four days while
the neighbours poured drinks and rolled dice while
I went for a job interview I wouldn't be called for while
your heart enjoyed its vacation while
your phone battery collapsed with you
two days in
to the rest of your life.

2.27.19
Mom talked to the man who found you.

The purple in his cheeks sings the hymns
she didn't let us. He sits stiff as a board and
recounts how your skin was a porcelain sea while Mom
is a pale forget-me-not.

5.6.18
You always said you felt forgotten. I'm sorry
you left in a dust storm, the world bustling, no one
realising you were a victim to the breeze. Not realising
you stopped breathing in the door
they always swept by.

2.28.19
How can your city be bitter
on my fingers?
How can a song feel dusty
on my tongue?

3.19.19
The night holds a knife to my throat, taking the flowers
I planted in the garden. In the morning, I start anew,
knowing my daisies will be gone by midnight. But why
do I try?
Why do I
try?

2.3.19

You always said you felt like a burden. I'm sorry
the phone lines sighed and the highways hummed
while you sank into your mattress, watching
from the sidelines, crying about why
no one was looking for you.

2.16.19

I touch your door and cry as the coffee brews upstairs.
The air feels colder down here than it used to, and I know
    that means you're at your desk,
    like you always were,
    fading through the chill.

7.13.19

I finish my novel as your urn
sits across from me,
reflecting the dedication—the girl
I wished to save.

8.3.18

You always said you felt,
and I'm sorry.

4.2.19

I turn twenty-one in a barricade.
I wish the sunset got me drunker.

0.0.00
I will tell you
what no one else will
about grief:
They grieve too.

2.7.19

The snow shifts on a bookmark,
dying on my desk, in a font
you would've hated anyway.

I will tell you what the world won't
about grief. It comes on February fifth,
2019, a blue Tuesday.
It comes wrapped in silk apologies
and a satin bag I'm
too afraid to open.
2.5.19

I don't think I'll ever find them

I can still feel your knife sliding
between my car keys and the gape
in my closet door. I can feel your ghost
in my living room and our hallway, pacing
the carpet where the wires I bought
sparked the life I built you. I search cupboards,
cabinets, and corners for the stolen
pieces of my puzzle. My drawers
are full of you, but empty of us.
I water the grass, praying for greenery,
but all I find are the wilted, fading
in your foggy sky.

I poisoned my soil, praying
someone would save my lilies,
but instead, everyone
watched my wilting petals and never
bothered to ask
why?

So, when people ask why
my garden is barren, I point to the polaroids
and ask, "Would they want it
any other way?" After all,
the keys to my car
are still missing.

bitter dreams

She is sunset. The end. The crashing of
a forced finale. We can only
pray that she rises
in the morning.

Autumn

The Warning in the Wallpaper

Dear Tuesday,

Today, the sun haunts the wallpaper, casting wisteria shadows. The trees faint. Their leaves fade like the fall. Everything feels colder in the fog. This is the ache of the year.

This is the dreamy decay, this is the collapse. The chill in your back, the twinkle in a hazelnut haven. Here, the dead are magic; the trees offer their hair as beds and roots as liberation. The age of summer dims and dies, and the world offers everything it can—to its dying breath—for me.

Just for me. This dawn of decay is my home.

The colours hug me in the wind, whipping at my heels and nails. The sidewalks have their ways of lulling me.

Autumn is winter's gatekeeper. Her decay is fierce and wild. She is ripe and gracious, loud and bewitched. We watch the earth burn to ash without the grace of a funeral.

But winter has come and gone. Its knife brushed my throat for many moons and tidings, and I know now why autumn is my favourite; her soul has been sacrificed for me. Sweet familiarity.

Light pierces the veil and attacks the bookcase, a morning ode from summer's mother. I wonder what she's trying to tell me, but I know.

I know.

It's getting colder. How will morning ever feel the same without the day peeking through cracks in the birch? Like a lifeline in the pavement? The blonde wisps in the sky are a sacrifice made for a new day.

It gets colder and colder.

All the way down we go.

Lost In The Leaves

She's a wisp of the wind,
and I'm a bottle of wine, aged
and staged
for kitchen-rack display.

Loud traffic fills my bedroom
from corners to window,
a city of life. This static
is never-seizing
and here, in my corner of
our holographic city, she is
one wisp in
a sea of wind.

How old am I
now? Has my cork
fallen in? Tainted me? This
crimson flush and my cracking glass,
this skin, these
are all
I have left.

My cork gives way to the sand, but
goodbyes are all
that pass through.

I am a cracked bottle, and she
is the summer breeze.
Disconnected from touch,
forgotten in the front lawn,
now we can fly
with the leaves.

can he hurt us any more

Will you love me through February?
It feels different come May than July.
I love in alien days, foreign times
scattering like dice across the border.
The table is set for
October's grey feast.
The clock cries; the bird, freed.
and the wails of time ache by.

And when I ask if you will love me
come shattering December
I already know the answer.
The game has been played, and the dice
lie in the palms of Atlantis.
January will fade
like a ghost in the snow.
time is a light switch, it flickers on
and then off.
And will I ever be
old enough to see the beating trees?
Our locked lips seal letters
addressed only to your gravel home
in the library.
Will I ever
be old enough?

In the striped news, she
is laid to rest. Calamity seeps in
from warm meals and long walks.
I can feel the burnt street lights
and lost birds in lieu of her.
She falls, vulnerable only
to herself and the sky.
a member of the grave-village,
buried in her shelter,
she is just
one more night
lost to tacenda.

Soul Sisters

"What would you say if your sister was still alive?"

That I understand. That I'm not mad. I've never been. Not when her funeral stole my lace armour. Not when Mom screamed, or Dad wailed. Not when I was left all alone to climb our promised mountains.

I'm not mad that she is gone.

I'm mad that she's been stolen.

A hostage of engouement, she was afraid. A blade held to her chest: her enemy. I'm mad that she fought for control, pummelling and scarring, but lost her grip.

She was so close to the summit,
but she slipped.

She knew her ropes were frayed. She knew her grip was faltering. Our hike is now my clamber. She didn't know how to warn me through the snow.

I'm mad the world viewed her through blue and bruised glasses. Trapped in scorned skin, she dreamed of taking to the sky.

I would tell my sister I'm not mad. That now, I hear her, feeling closer to the elevation. I would tell her I know that she has not abandoned me. I'll place her rosebuds in my pockets and her spirit in my backpack.

I would say, "You're finally no longer in pain. Don't worry.

I'll conquer this summit for the both of us."

game night

The leather was always cold,
red pain across the living room.
We played the game of their nature,
poisoned fruits from our
heirloom tree.
His cards snap beside my heart
on the table.
"Disappointments."
His own aces, beaten
by his spades and his clubs.

But the game was always meant
to be peaceful.

The couch once stung my back. A buzz
that would fade through
the carnations in my glass.
Game night, but never
the kind we liked.
Our deck of cards stacked
against the listing glass.
He plays his hand, rattling out the ash
as I'd always remembered.

But his touch was always meant
to be peaceful.

Now, there are dead roses
in the library, the same flush
as her life-lost cheeks, and his trials felt
like daggers through dust.
A decade adrift, now
I face his hand
alone.

the clock cries

I have my morning coffee too early
and my pills far too
late. I sit on fabrics that supported
my back and your shoulders; my hopes
and your guitar. I sit
with the snow and leaves, watching as
they dance for me; praying that
they will stay
like they promised.

I eat far too late and I dream
far too early. I sit with your
fabrications, pressing beside and into me.

I steal a stare of the highway, the snow
showing me their waltz, the leaves
kissing the mosaic sky,

and I wonder if our timing

ever mattered.

Tick Tick Tick

Love me blue and wild.
it's 8:03. A clock
clicks while he ticks. I watch
the feathers of futures flutter and
crack. the walls are as wooden
as they are hollow. I witness the dusk
of a dream at five
forty-three.
another click, another chip
on a shoulder I need to repair. Cement
works no longer. The cobblestone is salty,
and his ticks lull
impending time.
When I ask, just past eight,
if he will adore me in azure,
he ticks
like a bomb
as my answer.

Picnics in the Spring

She mixed her tea with honey, swirling,
in a China glass. Her smile is all lavender;
coaxing, hazy, seemingly
misplaced here.
And when I ask why her smile is
as ripe as the garden,
she wilts like
the shore sweeping through
our glasses.

I am mourning the ghost of an evening
that never was; her scorning
growing unwell. The grass is dead
around where she lays, and the trees
wonder why no one holds
their hands these days, but I
am longing for a loss that
has not happened yet.
It's began on the first day;
the sun kissed noon.

Full Pockets

I used to hate carrying spare change. Now,
more than pennies and quarters
pull me to the soil.

They are the anchors of trinkets I
can never give. When quarters replace
coffee runs and dimes replace
dinners, my jeans
keep me weighted
to the bottom
heavy with change.

I'm Watching the Sunset Without You

The memory is merely
a wounded song. A melodic
thought that's
just slightly out of touch.
Like whiskey, it aches when
the knife, at our height,
wedges its way
between
our fainting lines.
And then, suddenly,
our song simply
stops.

Foreign Goodbyes

He leaves before the coffee hits
the counter, and he's clocked
before my sugar jar hits
the floor. He's a ghost, a
vacancy I once cherished,
and now crave. Yet whenever I'd say
"You forgot to kiss me
goodbye" I fell
one step closer to his door.
He leaves before the sun
brushes my swollen cheeks,
and by then I will be
in his forlorn memory.

my new favourite word

Austice means "a
wistful omen of
the first sign of autumn."

Autumn is decay. The farewell
of my half, when my heart cracked
on the leaves, when my sister's blood
laced the calendar, when I was locked
within my ribs, when screams echoed
the upstairs hall, but none believed me
until they faded. It was when
we sparked our fire, brewing
before the winter killed us. It was the season
when I cried upstairs, hoping
my ricochet could climb.
I extended my prayers, limb by limb
for nothing but
a ghost of a grasp.

But since,
I've learned that austice
is my favourite season.

It's the one where I fell
and yet survived.

Summer

The Flames

Dear all of you,

> The common areas were my second choice, but
> her rosy walls were my haven. She always knew,
> scanning my depths while skimming the surface.
> Adorned lashes and crystal smiles,
> the clink of a dollar around my neck.
>
> The living room was never my first choice.
> It was anywhere that didn't smell lonely.
>
> "We don't spend enough time together."
> Her words fell through the wind, abandoned on my shoulders,
> shades of tattered greys and blues,
> before it even had a chance
> to breathe.
>
> Her door clicks and echoes,
> clouding over in the skies of our
> childhood treasure. I click at my foggy mind,
> cluttered with new days and
> old ruts.
>
> "Are you coming?"
> Her words are bruised, her soul

tattered from the passing sun, and me,
her only saviour,
lost in my own paradox.

The impending storms over me,
her bruised heart, discarded.
Her aching voice rests
on the sand bed of the sea.

"I already know what you're going to say."
Her aches were shoved in a kitchen drawer,
for junk and discarded misfits.

The kitchen was never my first choice.
Her breeze feels nothing like home.
And when her warm soothing light had
entered my chilled waters,
I think
I allowed her
to drown.

Leather haunts my skin, but
raven-stained jackets were always
her favourites. I've simmered in it,
the plastic and woven luxury.
The smell of smoke
fills the kitchen.
I think I now
finally understand.

"Meet you in the basement?"
"I'll be right there."

an ode to coffee dates

She loved her leather tattoos, and had
gold hair kissed by roses.
Glass to her lips, fizzy
and red, with a pineapple smile
and maroon boots, laced in secrets.

Her skin was screen-bleached and bruised,
from the way she clicked her fingers and
rolled her nails. She liked her coffee sliced,
sharp, melting in drained eyes
made for the sky.

Her fingers dance along buttons;
blood, ivory, me, and the angry sea,
warmth hugging the high.
"Ready?"
"You know it."

We kidnap the moon embodied in concrete,
a secret for her and me.
The sun is a whisper on the stairwell,
and she never leaves a drink unfinished.

The best part about our coffee dates
is that we never know when they're over.

The sacred hearts club, breakfast
on the midnight horizon. Her smile
is so yellow it blinds me.

Midnight At Noon

I am dizzied by the moon.
She is bright and loud, and calls to me
in faint, weak songs.
But the morning birds grow drunk
on frozen berries; fluttering and puttering,
dancing on dead leaves. The sun,
she's alive, sparking
beneath the grieving glass. I
am on a flatline elevation,
square one on our rusted chalkboard,
and the midnight sky burns
the oncoming grey.

I wish
more than ever
that I could fly.

A Chill on the Beach

And with these April sunsets
somehow I forget the
onset of winter. Of the fog that
coats the curtains and melts
the sidewalks. The ice is caked on
the walls of my soles
and the plans in my palms.
But, here in the sunset, the fire
melting away the coals of the day,
and I forget
to put on my sweater.

Mornings I Dread

Our souls make breakfast together.
Our mourning, like dew along the rails.
I make the coffee.
I hate it bitter, but you love it. You always
like it this way, just like you
love the gloom, but I fear it.

The shadows hold my ribs, the closet
can only lock so tight. My bones
shake, then sigh. It's always crisp.
You always liked it this way, the frost
swatting at my lashes and wrestling
with my air. This
is always.

My epiphany then melts
into my toast. My coffee tastes
stronger than usual,
but my tragedy hasn't reached
act three.

i didn't know

My peonies are bitter and
raw. Undercooked. Possibly
underfed. But that vibrant grass
that coated my cavern always
seemed so peaceful.
I didn't know they were toxic
until the storm.

A Fallen Crest

The willow-punch and pocket-bunch
are stuffed in the seams of my jeans.
I pluck and share them
with anyone in reach
of the hold. Childhood
bursting from my pockets.

One, stuffed with the flowers,
the other, her swollen crest.
Carrying blessings and brambles,
we dance through the grass.

The world is alive, but the backyard
hasn't bloomed the same
since the ice hatched a deal
with the flowers, and
since my branches died
in the driveway.

Chosen Family

My sister once bought me a bunny.

The clasp of winter had its palm in my back, guiding me through the weary wild. 2015 and seventeen, stealing kisses in the weeds. I made wishes on wells, but expected nothing. We are

a paralysed house of four, isolated at the sidewalk's end. There are twelve soles on our dusty doormat, and I know strangers have been climbing up our carpet. Up and up, heaven

must be closer than I thought.

Black, white, and gold. A treasure in a quirky cage, the roof not sitting quite right, but her home was a haven all the same. But when my sister bought me my bunny,

I didn't know it was a trade,

not a gift.

flames

Am I finally back on my meds?
Or are my hands just stained with red
from touching the truth with
a burning branch
and putting our treehouse
to sleep?

In Bloom

The ghosts of wisteria wisp my feet,
singing and snapping,
but this forlorn path leads me
out of the moor and into the fogs
that are running me to Rome.
Through the sea of Paris and
the lake-lined bedroom walls.
I can feel their wallpaper petals
reaching out to hold me.
Un bouton d'or, my dear,
and hello.

Spring

What You Are

My dear,

You are sacred. It may hurt to hear, but it's true.

You give your heart so willingly to the streets and the gutters that people assume it can be discarded. Downtown is a lonely place, and as the cars breeze and whip, you are frozen. But snow thaws and ice melts. The remnants of the season always fade. The seeds of spring are oncoming and wild.

But this concrete city is cold. Your heart sits at the crosswalk, watching passersby with golden tins and rummage bins. The world is a crossword with fences and barricades, but you stand. A survivor of the capture. A survivor of the charcoal streets that abolish the breathing like you.

But don't fear. The hauntings of midnight and daybreak only last so long, and survival was a fist-fought gift. Your heart is earned and relentless.

Your buds were sown in flower fields and the night sky. You were not made for the dewdney dives, you were made for the honeyed sugar hives. You may drown in it all, but you emerge on the shore.

This world is so loud and yet spring is so soft; the soft sanctuary after your survival. Remember that nook in the galaxy — to the right of the sun — where your memories sleep. When the streets are too fierce, the stars can call you home.

You are here. You have survived.

Welcome to spring, my dear new flower.

The garden is quiet and waiting.

Come on in, my love.

Angel Dreams

Ten a.m. on a Tuesday,
she is a whisper. But the clock
twirls and spins
before I know she is a bird.
She sings on my shoulders,
through lunches and exams,
my hazy raspberry dream.

(I will walk with you to home,
whenever, wherever
that may be.)

She slips through
the spring lilacs, and every song
is a secret from her just for me.
Through pink, perfumed lies, my saint
is a symphony, but also
only a lull in my day.

1:47am

Rachel,

Do you remember our breakfast at midnights? The jaded diner seats, the clink of liquor in the kitchen, and the smell of fresh pancakes and your laugh, filled with leather and French vanilla. It felt like Coca-Cola and vanilla, even

if I didn't savour them at the time.

We stitched hearts over brimming caffeine. She pulled her phone from her jacket, the chill infused with leather. Faux and fortunate, unlike her. We spilled leftovers in my car, egg whites on the floor. My plight was a giggling choir. Those strawberry highs felt so real when she was more

than just a memory.

"Refill?" Always.

The sun takes the corner, peeking her sweet head over the night's gloomy mist, but we will stay. Wrapped in cardigans and hope, breakfast never tasted so sweet. Leaving means our defences, shields armed, become china in the breeze. I hadn't known how sacred our booth was then, if only I'd caught the chance.

I carry breakfast shadows in my pockets and pull back my quill. Now, my silver linings have slipped out to sea. Nighttime approaches. Her tide dots the sky and byline, but my car

is silent. The seats are decaying grey, but this engine is the only diner where I am with her.

The neon signs are dimming goodnight, and my pocket of scarlet is all I have. But here, my cups are never empty. I savour the warmth of her ghost. The evening tide no longer our threat.

My passenger seat is forever reserved for you, even

if I no longer eat breakfast.

From my sweet pea

Dear Taylor,

I can't believe you're actually eighteen,
the age your soul was hijacked. Her paper is
stained with sincerity, and lined
with the pages of her notebook. I read it,
longing for sunlight. The storm clouds
have been hung, and I've forgotten
how to breathe,
and how to be.
With April's candlelight within our reach,
presents are back of mind.

This gift was the best to send with you.
It's capable of clutching anything, and time
is a precious prize. Our spilled midday laughter
and caffeine coated highs were
volcanic. This ash
is all we have left.

Your friends agreed to bring it to you
and blue plastic is
all I have left. It spits
hazy memories, all dressed
in framed golds. This static
is my only way

of reaching you.

There's more waiting for you at home
but home
is exactly
what I've been waiting for.
Her offering is now
a mausoleum,
for her
and for the tattered remnants
of me.

It didn't feel right
but you are safe, now. Free
from the cage of a heartbeat.
Dust settles on silent
keyboards, and the mahogany
still cries
on the basement floor.

My saint tells me to
make it special!
but special is alien
in a world of discipline.

I lay her words on my forearm
and steep her into my skin.
Her rarity is a scar I
put on display,

as not all wounds
are accidental.

Finally

Winter pleads: "Please,
can I stay outside just
five minutes more?" but spring
coos at her brilliance. The florals
hold her fingers like silk, and her hair
like paper. Spring speaks
to sooth the bitter wind.
"Your time here, just for now, is done.
Now, it is time for us
to start something new."

February

This chamomile breeze captures me, cradling
the hair she has grown and the silver
chained to her neck. They're found creeping
up through the snow banks, wistful
for the withdrawal. The jasmine drifts to sleep
in my tea, and the wind beats the glass
to be stained. But still, the lavender
starts to sing, and the birds rock perennials
to sleep, and I think February
won't be so bad after all.
The sunrises and the vines
have all told me so.

There is Freedom

My father will never hear me.
These thunder tidings rave and wage
and he never dares to look
my way.

I am dressed in Saturn,
dolled up and hollow,
cleaning and gliding,
hoping to be more
than a cork in a pond.

Our father can never hear me. When I cry
on the boardwalk couch, he
is already off at sea. And when she
hears my pleas
from the keel of her Achilles,
she closes the door.

But she cannot stand to hear me either.
Our lifeboats have been set
a-sail. The lucky ones that got away.

I am trapped
in their sinking skin
as the sunrise bobs at the surface

but father cannot see me.
And mother
cannot bear me.

The sailor's ode is adorned in Venus,
but I sit here, humming
at my bitter ends. The seas are still
but I am ready.
I'm all sewn up, Mars tucked
in my pocket.

She cannot see me, and he
cannot hear me. My life now belongs
to our waves.

I am no longer afraid.

Thank you for joining me.
Welcome to spring.

To learn more about how we can stop the opioid crisis, visit canada.ca/opioids
and encourage your local government representatives to support safe consumption sites
and harm reduction services.